PARLIAMENT BUILDINGS, STORMONT

The building, its setting, uses and restoration

1922 - 1998

UAHS

Ulster Buildings Series

Series Editor: Peter Rankin

Malone House 1983
Ballywalter Park 1985
Clandeboye 1985
Hillsborough Castle 1993
Parliament Buildings, Stormont 1999

First published 1999 by the
Ulster Architectural Heritage Society
66 Donegall Pass, Belfast BT7 1BU

Designed by Alison Gault
Typeset in Sabon
Printed by Nicholson & Bass Ltd

ISBN 0 900457 51 1

A catalogue record is available from the British Library

The publication of this book has been underwritten by
CONSARC DESIGN GROUP
KARL CONSTRUCTION LIMITED

Contents

It was a major tragedy when the Commons Chamber in Parliament Buildings, Stormont, was destroyed by fire in January 1995. Parliament Buildings, in their fine landscaped grounds, has been described as 'one of the most outstanding architectural sights in Ireland'. Within the dignified neo-classical exterior are some very grand interior spaces, and one of these was the Commons Chamber.

After the fire it emerged that there were very inadequate records of the details of the Chamber on which to base a reconstruction. It was therefore decided to commission an archaeological excavation to recover all the information which this rigorous approach could produce. The results of this 'fire archaeology' informed the restoration, together with all the other sources of evidence.

The Commons Chamber was originally built to a very high specification, using elaborate materials, and the restoration work demanded enormous care and very high standards. All those involved in the restoration work are to be warmly congratulated - architects, engineers, craftsmen of all kinds and many others. This book will serve as a fitting record of their achievement in restoring one of the finest rooms in Parliament Buildings. The Commons Chamber and the rest of this great building are now ready for their new uses into the next millennium.

Lord Dubs
Minister for the Environment

INTRODUCTION

DOE CONSTRUCTION SERVICE

Parliament Buildings is recognised in Northern Ireland and beyond as one of our great architectural set pieces. Its elegant features and grand setting together with some fine interior apartments place upon us all a duty of care for the benefit of this and future generations. Planning for the general refurbishment needed after almost 60 years of use was commenced in 1985.

In 1991 we were appointed to project manage a limited refurbishment, primarily to address aged and decayed services installations and the requirements of revised construction legislation. However, as the project developed it was evident that significant structural restoration and modernisation would also be necessary. The tragic fire of 2 January 1995, which totally destroyed the former Commons Chamber, brought additional challenges for the Professional Team not only to ensure accuracy in the restoration when virtually no records existed, but also to develop the necessary structural changes in a manner in keeping with Sir Arnold Thornely's interpretation of the Greek classical style.

Elsewhere the opportunity was taken to detail new apartments in a contemporary classical style and to add character and quality to the building's exterior appearance through extensive hard landscaping and lighting.

We are naturally proud to have led this historic restoration through to completion and to have shared with our professional colleagues from the private sector, with contractors and the many specialist crafts and trades in restoring and preparing this splendid building for a new century.

In the early 1990s Parliament Buildings had become tired and weary. Much of its original quality and integrity was compromised and obscured by numerous ad-hoc alterations and temporary additions. It was, in many respects, unloved and the parliamentary accommodation lay unused.

We started work on the building in 1991, planning a comprehensive refurbishment to suit modern office needs, but it was the fire of 1995 that reinvigorated the will for full restoration and adaptation for new uses.

From the start, the challenge was to adopt the building to provide new office, parliamentary and hospitality accommodation, yet sensitively to restore the major historic spaces and protect the character of the building. This developed into a 'twin track' policy - accurate and sensitive restoration of the valuable original fabric, such as the Members' Dining Room; and a contemporary yet complementary design ethos for completely new spaces, such as the 'Long Gallery'. It is an approach which respects and pays homage to the old, yet marks down the alterations as of their own time.

We were intimately involved in every aspect of the restoration, working closely as a team with DOE Construction Service and BDP Mechanical and Electrical Engineers and ultimately with Karl Construction. We are immensely proud of our efforts and recognise it as a unique experience where we could contribute to a symbolic and practical renaissance of perhaps, the most important building in Northern Ireland.

Karl Construction feel privileged to have been the main contractors for the complete restoration of Parliament Buildings, Stormont.

The project proved to be a complex task, demanding both sensitivity to the character of the original and effective management in order to ensure that the work was completed to the highest standard in the most efficient manner.

We are pleased to pay tribute to the quality of not just our own workforce, but those of the dozens of specialist contractors who worked on aspects of the job. The vast majority of the work was carried out by local people, proving that the skills and expertise of the past are still there and can respond to the challenge being set. Stone carving, gilding, intricate joinery, marble and terrazzo, fibrous plaster, cast bronze, all were carried out by Northern Ireland craftsmen and craftswomen.

The restoration of Parliament Buildings was an intense experience which went far beyond a normal construction job. We are honoured to have been able to refurbish and equip this building for the next century.

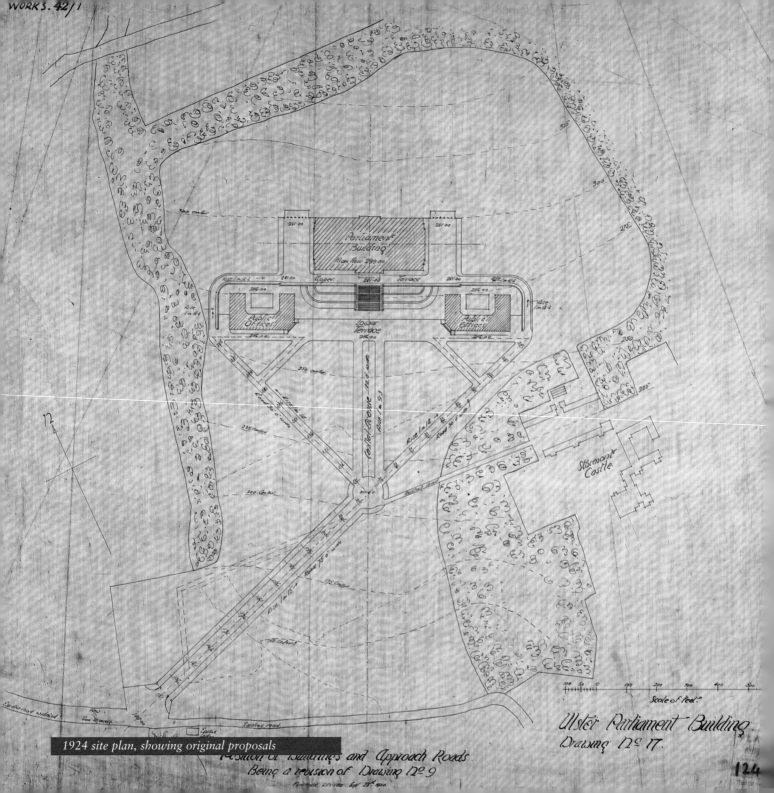

1924 site plan, showing original proposals

Ulster Parliament Building
Drawing No. 17.

124

Position of Buildings and Approach Roads.
Being a revision of Drawing No. 9

PART 1

ARCHITECTURAL & PARLIAMENTARY HISTORY

1. The search for Parliament Buildings

2. Design, construction & setting, 1922 - 1932

3. The building in use, 1931 - 1998

1. THE SEARCH FOR PARLIAMENT BUILDINGS

Following the Government of Ireland Act of 1920 Belfast gained an unexpected status as a provincial capital. It suddenly needed to acquire such appurtenances of statehood as a parliament house, headquarters buildings for government departments and a high court of justice, the first two of which concern us here. The administrative and parliamentary headquarters had to be sufficiently imposing to establish the identity of the new administration to the world outside Northern Ireland and to its own citizens. So an appropriate building with debating chambers suitable for two houses of parliament, committee rooms, library and dining rooms had to be supplied.

The City Hall and Assembly's College

It was necessary to find a temporary home for the Parliament quickly. The inauguration of the Parliament on 22 June 1921 by King George V and its first full session the following day took place in the City Hall. Belfast Corporation, long the second municipality in Ireland and one of the major city governments in the United Kingdom in a great age of local government, did not welcome what it saw as a rival to its authority, so the Parliament almost immediately found other premises. (It was briefly to return to the City Hall in the autumn of 1932 for the last sessions before the opening of Parliament Buildings).

From September 1921 until June 1932 Parliament met in Assembly's College in Botanic Avenue, Belfast (now Union Theological College), the theological college of the Presbyterian Church in Ireland. The Presbyterian Church was the most substantial all-Ireland body to be centred on Belfast and so one of the few to have buildings there on the 'national' scale required for a parliament. An annual rent of £8,000 was paid for use of the College. This period, during which the Parliament established its character as a legislative body, was commemorated by the bookplate used by the Parliamentary Library until the dissolution of Parliament in 1973. The offices of the new ministries were established in various rented premises round Belfast city centre.

11

Choosing the Site

The selection of a permanent site was quickly made. Three sites in or near the city, at Belfast Castle, Orangefield and Belvoir Park, were looked at and rejected. Another option available, but not seriously considered, was the outright purchase of Assembly's College. At the same time Stormont Castle and its surrounding demesne came on the market. On 20th September 1921 the Parliament of Northern Ireland voted its approval of the Stormont Castle demesne as *'the place where the new Parliament Houses and Ministerial Buildings shall be erected and as the place to be determined as the seat of the Government of Northern Ireland as and when suitable provision has been made therefor'.*

This approval was necessary as, under the terms of the Government of Ireland Act 1920, the seat of Parliament was to be in Belfast unless Parliament chose differently. At the time Stormont was outside the city boundaries, although they were later extended to include it. The Commissioners of Public Works and Buildings of the Imperial Government purchased the estate and house for £20,334 in December 1921.

12

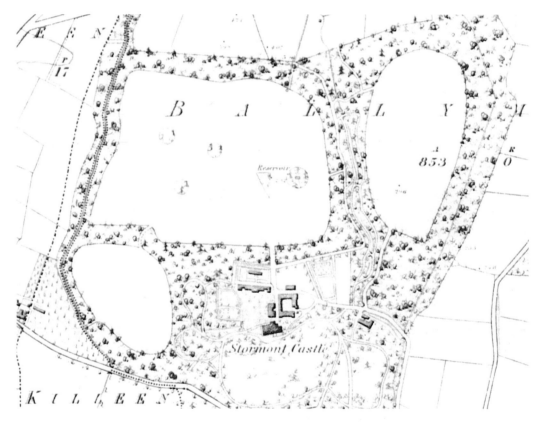

The Cleland estate from the 1860 Ordnance Survey

Stormont Estate

The present Stormont estate is superimposed upon a modest demesne, established, as a result of an advantageous marriage and reputedly ill-gotten gains, by the Rev. John Cleland in the early years of the nineteenth century. It lay on a well-drained, south-facing slope, with three deep glens. Cleland did not further his reputation by gating the road from Belfast to Groomsport, which ran across his land. Part of the road can still be seen today, near the present Massey Avenue entrance and delineated by Irish yews.

The 1830 house, Storm Mount, described just after it was built as a '…large plain house with very little planting about it', was eventually enhanced by an orchard and a shelter belt of trees growing to the south-west. Neighbouring properties, including sizeable Rose Park, were acquired, farmland was developed and extensive woodland shelter planted as the century progressed. The Ordnance Survey map of 1860, and photographs taken in the 1890s, show a well-wooded demesne surrounding the house, which had been enlarged in 1858 for Cleland's grandson and namesake and had by then assumed the appropriate title of Stormont Castle. The exterior was re-designed to the fashionable Scottish Baronial style by the local architect Thomas Turner, possibly based on earlier plans by one of the leading country-house architects of the day, William Burn. Cladding of Scrabo stone was added to the plain house, with crenellations and turrets topped by fearsome gryphons. This was complemented by a terraced garden, including a complex lay-out of flower beds. A fine, and surviving, lean-to glasshouse was backed by bothies, offices and stove house. The walled kitchen garden has now gone, but the stables remain.

The Cleland family finally left in 1893, preferring to live abroad, and the demesne was let out. On the departure of the tenant, initial efforts to sell failed, but fortunately the newly-formed Northern Ireland Parliament was seeking a site for parliament buildings and purchased the holding which amounted to 235 acres, including 100 acres of woodland.

Over a period of ninety years the landscape had changed from one of small farm units to a single well-managed demesne, with ornamental and productive gardens at the house; fields, woodland and parkland; and the inevitable wet land at the bottom of the hill.

The house was saved from demolition by pressure of local opinion and was utilised from 1922 until 1940 as the official residence of the first Prime Minister, Sir James Craig, and subsequently as offices for the Prime Minister and the Cabinet Office. During the period of direct rule from Westminster it accommodated the office of the Secretary of State for Northern Ireland. Unfortunately the gate lodge, formerly belonging to Rose Park and re-modelled in c.1860 by Thomas Turner, was demolished in 1962 to make way for the approach to Dundonald House, a government building erected in the grounds at that time.

Stormont Castle. Rear view from north west, c.1894

2. DESIGN, CONSTRUCTION & SETTING, 1922 - 1932

Even by modern standards the design and construction of Parliament Buildings was an immense task, comparable today with the new Parliament for Scotland which has a budget over £50m. The building was to be the gift of the Imperial Government and was constructed under the supervision of the Board of Works, responsible to the Treasury at Whitehall for expenditure, which eventually amounted to a total cost of £1.2m. After a limited competition, the Board of Works appointed Arnold Thornely FRIBA of Liverpool as the architect in 1922. Thornely, of Briggs and Thornely, was also responsible for the Preston Municipal Building (1930) and for Warrington Town Hall. He was knighted for his work on Stormont in 1932.

The construction process could be set out as a simple catalogue of dates:

March 1923	Site preparation started.
19 May 1928	Foundation stone laid by the Governor of Northern Ireland, the Duke of Abercorn.
May 1931	Initial occupation of the building.
16 November 1932	Opening ceremony performed by the Prince of Wales (later King Edward VIII).
22 November 1932	First Parliamentary session in the new building commenced.

17

The laying of the foundation stone of Parliament Buildings by the Duke of Abercorn in 1928

SOUTH ELEVATION

Proposed design for New Parliament Building

However these simple facts disguise immense complexity, as described through the contemporary account in *The Builder*, for November 1932 :

> *It was the intention originally* [1922] *to divide the work into three separate blocks, the central building* [by Arnold Thornely] *being the Parliament House with a tower and dome while on a lower terrace two office blocks* [by Ralph Knott of London] *were to be built to accommodate civil servants. Excavation work was completed and the foundations laid (including that for the central dome, a 7' thick concrete slab thickened to 11' at the edges) before the demon cost came on the scene* [November 1925] *with the result that the two office blocks, tower and dome had to be abandoned.*
> *Mr. Thornely thereupon prepared a new design for a four storey building to suit the foundations already laid and providing accommodation for both parliamentary and office requirements.*

Behind this published account were months of wrangling between a Treasury determined to keep a limit on costs and Northern Ireland Government officials trying to accommodate increasing numbers of civil servants. The pamphlet *The truth about Stormont* published by the *Irish News* in January 1933, presents the opposition view of the construction of Parliament Buildings with an attack on what it saw as extravagance.

The cost was stoutly defended by Sir James Craig to the House of Commons as "not too costly to carry, and at the same time is of sufficient character to distinguish our Northern Parliament" and, a month later he praised the project as able to "absorb as many of the out-of-work as possible, and especially those ex-Service men who are now in a very sad state".

The Builder was warm in its praise of the design of the building, with a strong justification of its Greek Classical style as providing the required level of "the dignity associated with Parliament" and "an excellent example of the modern use of ancient art".

It is generally accepted that Thornely succeeded in both siting and design, taking full advantage of the elevated location and creating a well proportioned, dignified and impressive building, of Portland lime-stone resting on a plinth of unpolished Mourne granite. The hill-top background of dark trees both absorbs and sets off the substantial dimensions - 365 feet long, 164 feet deep and 70 feet high rising to 92 feet at the centre of the main façade.

Viewing the building from a distance, the effect produced by the well-proportioned masses, the central colonnaded and crested portico and the less elaborate but equally effective wings rising from a rusticated plinth, is very striking, and on a closer inspection intricate detail work on the strings and cornices and around the windows may be appreciated.

The first floor is treated as the 'piano nobile' with consoled cornices and balconies to certain windows, and as the base of the great Ionic columns and plain pilasters which rise through the ashlar of the first, second and third floors.

Above the central tetrastyle Ionic portico on the south elevation, Britannia and her lions crown the attic storey, but it is the sculpture group in the tympanum that has the greatest significance. It has been claimed to represent either Britain presenting the lighted torch of liberty to Northern Ireland, or Northern Ireland offering the flame of loyalty to the Crown. Although most of the external carved detailing follows strict classical patterns, the frequent use of the Irish Elk motif (modelled on the buchranium or ox's skull) is a unique feature. The sculpture and carving were by Malcolm Miller and Rendal Bond of Earp Hobbs and Miller of Manchester.

Construction

The construction was carried out in a total of fourteen separate contracts, all of which (except for tree-felling and levelling) were carried out by Stewart & Partners Ltd.

John Stewart started in business as a building contractor in Belfast in 1874. The firm expanded, and the founder's son, William J. Stewart, opened offices in Dublin and London, the latter becoming the headquarters of Stewart & Partners Ltd. In May 1929 W. J. Stewart was elected as MP for South Belfast, and re-elected unopposed in 1931.

21

The firm also built the Royal Courts of Justice in Chichester Street, Belfast, the other new essential building for the fledgling Northern Ireland state, to the design of James G. West.

The Stormont Parliament House and Administrative Buildings as originally planned

Photographs taken during the construction process
Left: Foundation trench and mini railway 1924. Top right: Foundations nearing completion
Bottom right: Road layout in progress

Belfast is largely a city of brick with a minimal stoneworking tradition. The commemorative volume issued by Stewart & Partners, records that the Portland stone was "required at a rate never before demanded in Ireland". Random blocks were shipped from Portland to Belfast, and at the height of the contract 1600 cubic feet of dressed stone were placed a week, with a total of 135,000 cubic feet used in all.

Against the spirit of the times (evident at the contemporary Royal Courts of Justice), Parliament Buildings is of solid masonry construction (stone and brick) with the only steel framing being in the two debating Chambers and the Central Hall. As the contractors pointed out, this meant that they were unable to adopt the "modern practice of proceeding with concrete floors, brickwork and stonework at various points and levels simultaneously and the construction was governed by the rate stone was available and could be laid and the roof could not be completed until the walls were full height".

However, other modern techniques and ideas were incorporated - for example, floors and ceilings heated by hot water pipes embedded in the concrete flooring system.

West elevation:- the stonework reaches the third floor

With the re-design of November 1925 came a promise of completion within three and a half years. This proved optimistic as the foundations for the revised building were not ready until the summer of 1926. It took a further year to build the basement storey, and it was not until May 1928 that the structure reached ground level and the 'foundation stone' could be 'laid'.

The Northern Ireland Cabinet had invited the Prince of Wales to perform the task after it was realised in 1923 that the more traditional 'cutting the first sod' would be impractical, the condition of the site precluding a ceremonial party. In the event the Prince of Wales was not available and it was the Governor of Northern Ireland, the Duke of Abercorn, who pressed the switch on the electric hoist that lowered the stone into position.

Within it is a sealed casket containing, amongst other items, copies of the London *Times* and several local newspapers, a volume of the Northern Ireland Hansard and a collection of coinage.

By early 1931 the superstructure was completed, and in May the first civil servants started to move in. The fitting out of the Parliamentary accommodation, particularly the debating Chambers, continued, and on 16 November 1932 the building was formerly opened by the Prince of Wales. The first Parliamentary session commenced less than a week later on 22 November.

The Interior

The layout of Parliament Buildings is dominated by the three great ceremonial spaces of the Central Hall, the Commons Chamber and the Senate Chamber, all in the core of the building, separated by lightwells and surrounded by a perimeter of assorted offices. The main entrance is on the south front, but there are also imposing entrances on the east and west fronts, all marble lined and exquisitely detailed.

There is a surprising lack of either British or Irish symbolism in the interior detailing, which is almost exclusively based on strict Greek classical motifs.

The **Central Hall**, directly behind the main south entrance, is a double height space 100 feet long and 48 feet wide with galleries on all sides and is the "most sumptuous apartment in the building".

The floor is finished in cream, golden and walnut travertine marble, laid in a pattern reflecting the ceiling layout. The walls are panelled in cream travertine with intricate and masterly carvings, which throughout the building, are by Purdy and Millard of Belfast. The impressive central imperial staircase, in travertine with fine bronze balustrades, rises on both sides to the galleries leading, on the left, to the public gallery of the Commons Chamber and, on the right, to that of the Senate Chamber. On the dividing landing stands a bronze statue of Lord Craigavon, Northern Ireland's first Prime Minister, by L. S. Merrifield, of Chelsea, commissioned in 1938 but because of the War not installed until 1945.

26

The Central Hall as constructed
The Commons Chamber is to the left, the Senate Chamber to the right

The Hall is dominated by a majestic coffered ceiling with classical Greek motifs (though some seem more Egyptian in style) and heavily gilded by Heaton, Tabb & Co. of London, who were also responsible for the ceilings in the Senate and Commons Chambers. It is recorded that a special waxing process was applied to protect it against dust and dirt.

The focal point of the ceiling is the central chandelier from Windsor Castle, weighing a third of a ton. It was originally a gift to King Edward VII from his cousin Kaiser Wilhelm of Germany - the imperial German eagle is still visible on the boss. During the first World War the connection was thought unsuitable, and George V removed it from Windsor Castle into storage, until giving it to the Government of Northern Ireland. The other chandeliers are scaled down reproductions made for Parliament Buildings.

The *Senate Chamber* also rises through two stories and remains today largely as it was built. It was designed to seat 26 senators facing each other across the central 'table' and presided over by the Speaker sitting in an elaborate canopied chair. Flanking the Chamber are single storey division or voting lobbies. The Chamber's political life was limited, although in recent times it has been used as a committee room. It is an ornate and beautiful space, if perhaps a little staid in character. The bottocino marble walls are relieved by Irish linen and artificial silk damask panels. The official files (November 1929) record that these panels were deliberately kept plain "to afford an opportunity later for donation of tapestry etc. by some generous person".

Fluted Ionic columns in 'ebonised mahogany' delineate the window bays at first floor level and frame the galleries at each end. Above the public gallery are three painted arabesques symbolising the important industries of 1930s Ulster - linen, ship building and agriculture.

Linking the Senate Chamber to the Central Hall is an elegant circular lobby with a fine shallow-domed plaster ceiling and marble walls, repeated on the west side of the Hall on the approach to the Commons Chamber.

The **Commons Chamber** is also a double height space but larger than the Senate. It was built with press and public galleries at either end and formally laid out in Westminster adversarial style with the Government and Opposition facing each other across the central table in front of the elaborate Speaker's chair. As originally designed it seated 52 elected members plus officials. Proceedings were controlled by the Speaker, who was elected by the members from among their own number. The Chamber is flanked along the length of each side by single-storey division or voting lobbies. Above is the heavily moulded coffered ceiling, again classically detailed. The lower walls had superbly-matched walnut panelling, while the panelling above was of stone (travertine and 'manumarble') relieved by walnut window surrounds and by demi-columns with gilded Corinthian capitals. The joinery and woodwork in both Parliamentary Chambers was by Waring and Gillow, with the members benches and seats by Messrs J. P. White.

30

Left: The Commons Lobby, leading from the Central Hall to the Chamber
Top right: The Commons Chamber as originally constructed, with straight benches, Westminster style
Bottom right: The Members' Conference Room on the first floor

The remainder of the ground floor of the building is taken up by the Parliamentary accommodation - mainly grand offices off the stone-panelled corridors. The *Library* and *Writing* and *Reading Rooms* are arranged at the rear along the north façade and are the epitome of hushed dignity with a 'gentleman's club' aura, highly polished walnut bookcases, cork floors and deep leather armchairs.

Adjoining was the *Vote Office* where Members were issued with all the papers they needed for their parliamentary business.

31

Toilet accommodation is rarely the scene of architectural statements, and most washrooms at Parliament Buildings were in white glazed brick finishes with a utilitarian atmosphere.

However, in the Members' washrooms and the smaller visitors' washrooms on the ground floor, the opportunity was taken for a startlingly 'modern', even 'art deco' treatment. The walls were clad in black and grey 'vitrolite' opaque glass panels; the vanity basins and cubicle dividers were in black slate; the window linings in white marble, and the fittings in gleaming chrome.

The first floor is dominated by the *Members' Dining Room* behind the great balcony on the front elevation, oak panelled and floored, with the adjoining and linked *Conference Room*. Next to the Dining Room were a serving kitchen - an odd choice for such a prominent position on the front of the building - and the *Strangers' Dining Room*, a much more modest affair, deemed suitable for lesser mortals.

The rest of the first floor is taken up by Parliamentary offices, also grand and dignified, though the stone panelled corridors of the ground floor have here given way to plaster finishes.

The remaining floors were for civil service accommodation and are much more plainly finished, though still elegant with classical detailing and with a good quality of natural light. All the staircases are in travertine with bronze painted cast iron balustrading and bronze handrails, by Walter Macfarlane & Co. of Glasgow. The fourth floor (originally just the central area) housed the main kitchen and staff dining rooms. Within a few years of opening a series of lightweight wings had been placed on the roof, set on a grid of beams straddling the main walls.

The basement (or semi-basement, as high level windows at ground level give natural light to most rooms) was occupied by plant rooms and stores opening directly up the north 'slope' onto the rear access roadway. The road was cut into the rising hill behind and faced with an elegant Portland stone and brick retaining wall, with classical pavilions to each side.

The Imperial Staircase in the Central Hall

The Setting

The elegance of the building's composition in its setting should not be underestimated: visible shining on the hill from much of the city, it provides a series of dramatic vistas. The straight-on 'Prince of Wales' approach is perhaps the most impressive but the Massey Avenue tangent offers surprise and delight. From the east, the view of the portico and attic storey rising over the trees and contrasting with the Scottish baronial turrets of Stormont Castle is both tantalising and exciting.

The beautifully landscaped setting was specifically conceived on a grand scale to enhance the building, which, facing south-west, is high up on a terrace cut into rising ground and is framed by mature trees growing behind on the summit of the hill and by broad lawns below, which are flanked on either side by wide bands of greenery. A double lime avenue sharply defines the straight processional drive that ascends for some 180 feet over a distance of nearly a mile from entrance gates to the south, past the statue of Lord Carson, standing 32 feet high on level ground, and on up to the 90-foot wide granite steps which rise to the central doors of the building. The upper part of the avenue is edged effectively with eye-catching dark fastigate trees. Radiating roads lead from the statue at the epicentre : to the Massey Avenue entrance gates to the west; to Stormont Castle to the east; and to either side of the building, where wings were originally intended to be added.

Parliament Buildings rising behind the Scottish baronial turrets of Stormont Castle

The architect, Arnold Thornely, designed the handsome gates, gate screens, pillars, lamp standards and the lodges for both the Upper Newtownards Road and Massey Avenue entrances as part of the whole unified scheme. He included a building for a branch of the former Provincial Bank of Ireland, completed in 1932, which lies outside the estate but is integrated by an extended gate screen curving past it into Massey Avenue. The planning of the planting for the processional avenue, later named the 'Prince of Wales Avenue' is also attributed to the architect. False perspective was created by widening the space between the parallel rows of trees at the northern end. Red-twigged lime trees, Tilia platyphyllos 'Rubra' were chosen on the advice of W. J. Bean, curator of the arboretum at the Royal Botanic Gardens, Kew. All 305 trees survive today, having been continuously and successfully managed. Irish yews, Taxus baccata 'Fastigiata', were chosen for the upper avenue but have not faired so well on the higher and exposed site. Bean was also responsible for the pine clumps on the hillocks to the south.

Below Parliament Buildings, to the east, the oldest surviving Cleland trees remain in the vicinity of the red-brick Queen Anne style Stormont House which was originally built to accommodate the Speaker of the House of Commons. This was added in 1926 to designs by Knott and Collins of London. The Cleland home, Stormont Castle, was originally designated as the official residence for the Prime Minister. It was sidelined in the new plan, which also necessitated culverting streams, re-seeding former farmland and cutting through tree belts. Fortunately a considerable number of trees planted in the latter half of the nineteenth century remain and continue to enhance the site. Notable trees added since the creation of the present estate include a group of cedars presented in memory of the 36th Ulster Division and commemorative planting carried out by members of the Royal Family in 1951 and 1953.

Parliament Buildings from the air, before the restoration
Note the later roof level additions and the security hut on the east façade, both now removed

Since 1932 the Estate Superintendent has supervised maintenance. Horticulture advice and expertise were provided for many years by H. Armytage-Moore of Rowallane and much of his influence can be seen in the decorative section which lies between the westerly glen and the Massey Avenue entrance, where groups of ornamental flowering shrubs and trees flourish. A special feature of this area is the stone statue of a woman, engraved, 'THRIFT IS THE GLEANER BEHIND ALL HUMAN EFFORT' by the Belfast sculptor, John Knox, and dated 1951.

Carson's prominent statue in bronze is by L.S. Merrifield. To the east of Parliament Buildings, a sarcophagus of dressed Portland stone marks the tomb of Lord Craigavon who died in 1940. It was designed by R. Ingleby Smith, Chief Architect to the Northern Ireland Ministry of Finance, but not installed until 1942.

By 1955 the condition of some areas was giving cause for concern, and W. M. Campbell, curator at Kew Gardens, advised on felling and draining projects in the damp sectors on either side of the avenue. This was followed in 1968 by a full survey by Derek Lovejoy & Partners; one result of which was the re-inforcing of the yew rows in the upper avenue with Chamaecyparis lawsoniana. However, a suggestion to add a central lake was not taken up! The need for an overall management plan and assessment of priorities led to reports on all aspects of the landscape from 1984. Nature conservation has been a priority during the last decade, and depletion in the woodland has been checked by the on-going planting of native species. As part of the refurbishment of Parliament Buildings during the 1990s, the layout and planting in its immediate vicinity has been sympathetically designed by Mansil Miller.

The holding has been gradually increased over the years, beginning in 1929 with the acquisition of more land to the south for the main avenue. In 1956 and 1967 land was added on the eastern side and to the west in 1964/5. Three more fields were subsequently taken in, and at the end of the twentieth century the full extent covers 407 acres.

The Stormont estate accommodates many diverse buildings that have been added at different times. It is a workplace that necessitates traffic movement and parking spaces. It is also a public amenity as an attractive park. More recently it has become acknowledged as a wild-life preserve, offering a variety of habitats. Despite these pressures, the original plan of the formal setting for the focal point of the important public building has not been lost and remains thoroughly satisfactory.

3. THE BUILDING IN USE 1931-1998

Since its completion Parliament Buildings has functioned as the seat of a legislature, or other elected body when such have been in existence, and also as headquarters offices for various Government departments.

Use by Parliamentary Bodies

The Parliament of Northern Ireland had two chambers, a House of Commons and a Senate. The House of Commons had 52 members. Until 1969 these included four representatives from Queen's University. The Senate had 26 members, 24 of whom were elected by the Commons, with the Lord Mayor of Belfast and the Mayor of Londonderry as ex-officio members. The Government of Northern Ireland was chosen from the members of the majority party. The Parliament sat in Parliament Buildings for the first time on 22 November 1932. The last Parliament was prorogued on 30 March 1972 and abolished on 18 July 1973 by the Westminster Government.

The first Northern Ireland Assembly was elected on 28 June 1973 and sat for the first time on 31 July 1973. It had one chamber of 78 members. An Executive made up from Assembly Members of the Ulster Unionist, Social Democratic and Labour, and Alliance Parties took office on 1 January 1974. This Assembly was prorogued on 29 May 1974 and dissolved on 28 March 1975.

The Northern Ireland Constitutional Convention was elected on 1 May 1975 and met for the first time on 8 May 1975. Like the Assembly, it had 78 members who met under the Chairmanship of Sir Robert Lowry, Lord Chief Justice of Northern Ireland (now Lord Lowry). Set up under the Northern Ireland Act 1974, its specific remit was to consider what provision for the government of Northern Ireland was likely to command the most widespread acceptance throughout the community. It was then to report to the Secretary of State for Northern Ireland. The Convention produced a report which was judged by the Westminster Government not to have a sufficient degree of acceptance to warrant implementation and it was dissolved on 6 March 1976.

The next Northern Ireland Assembly was elected on 20 October 1982. Like the previous Assembly and Convention, it consisted of one chamber with 78 members. It had two main functions; to produce a scheme of devolution which would be adopted if backed by 55 of its members; and, through a committee system, to scrutinise the work of Government Departments. It met for the first time on 11 November 1982. This second Assembly was dissolved on 23 June 1986.

Subsequently Parliament Buildings was used as a base for the all-party talks in 1980 and in 1991 and 1992.

Under the terms of the Belfast Agreement of 10 April 1998 (now commonly known as the Good Friday Agreement) a Northern Ireland Assembly was elected on 25 June 1998. It sat for the first time in Parliament Buildings on 14 September 1998. An Executive is to be elected from its members by a system of proportional representation. It is intended that initially it should shadow the work of Government with full devolution taking effect in the early months of 1999. At the time of writing (November 1998) only the First Minister and Deputy First Minister have been elected.

42

Administrative Use

The original intention of the design of Parliament Buildings was to house the Ministries in wings at the sides. Because of cost this idea was abandoned, and the civil service was housed on the upper floors. For much of the building's life there was limited contact between the parliamentary and administrative organisations, each having its own entrance.

In 1931 all the Northern Ireland Government Departments moved into Parliament Buildings, with the exception of the Ministry of Commerce. (It was felt that this should be closer to the heart of Ulster business life, in Belfast city centre). Patrick Shea, later Permanent Secretary of the Ministry of Education, vividly describes in his autobiography the atmosphere of those early days:

We were a young service, not overworked and carefree. Young women were coming into the service in numbers and their presence brightened the scene. During the lunch hour on a summer's day the spacious grounds of Stormont had something of the atmosphere of a leisurely university campus. We talked about sport and the cinema, criticised our betters, explored the estate and watched, without enthusiasm, the coming and going of members of the Houses of Parliament.

It is important to remember that the Northern Ireland Civil Service was at that time small and had not experienced the enormous expansion in both its duties and its workforce that came about as the result of the arrival of the welfare state in the late 1940s.

Dr John Oliver, another former Permanent Secretary, describes his experience thus:

The way in which the work is done has changed since I entered the Service. The pace has increased. Public interest in the substance of our work and in the way we do it has intensified enormously. And the publicity that surround our activities has increased out of all recognition.

Extra office space was added on the fourth floor in 1935, but the Civil Service grew beyond the ability of Parliament Buildings to accommodate it. The Ministry of Finance, later the Department of Finance and Personnel, has had its headquarters in Parliament Buildings for most of its life. The Department of the Environment and the departments which preceded it were also based there until the completion of Clarence Court, its new headquarters building in central Belfast in 1993.

44

The Senate Chamber
View from the Public Gallery (west end) towards the Speaker's Chair and Press Gallery above

Parliament Buildings in Wartime

During the second World War the entire building was covered in dark camouflage paint, and part of it was taken over by the Royal Air Force. On 29 July 1941 the members of the Senate agreed in secret session to hand over the Senate Chamber for use as an Operations Room. From 25 September 1941 No.82 Group, Fighter Command, was based there. In October 1942 the Royal Air Force in Northern Ireland moved its headquarters into Parliament Buildings. In February 1945, as the war in Europe drew to a close, the RAF restored the Senate Chamber to the Parliament of Northern Ireland. A carved inscription in the face of the press balcony balustrade records the use of the Chamber as the Royal Air Force operations room during the second World War.

The Commons Chamber, pre fire, but with seating adjusted into a 'horse shoe' shape for the 1973 Assembly

PART 2

RESTORATION, REFURBISHMENT & ALTERATIONS, 1995 - 1998

1. FIRE

The fire of 1995 & its aftermath

2.10am January 2nd 1995

A strange smell was reported but the watchman's inspection revealed nothing.

9.00am January 2nd 1995

Daylight revealed smoke rising up the lightwells on either side of the Commons Chamber. The Fire Brigade was called, to discover an inferno in the Chamber and smoke filling the building.

Unsurprisingly, given the status of the building, conspiracy theories of terrorist attack were rife, but the subsequent forensic investigation revealed a simple electrical fault amongst the control systems buried beneath the Speaker's Chair. A slow-burning but deep-seated fire had followed, but the building's design and construction funnelled the fire through windows into the lightwells and thus minimised damage. The Chamber itself was totally burnt out but the adjoining rooms and corridors, though heavily smoke stained, survived surprisingly unscathed.

A major damage limitation exercise was initiated: everything was left as undisturbed as possible, and an archaeological salvage team was employed. They spent six weeks carefully sifting through the debris, cataloguing and labelling. Anything recognisable was placed in a special store to become the resource base for the restoration.

The Commons Chamber January 1995, immediately after the fire

At this stage it came to light that detailed drawings of the Chamber could not be found. The original building contract drawings were available but, as the Chamber was fitted out under a separate, later, contract, they showed only a blank shell. Subsequently, detailed furniture drawings were located at the Public Record Office in Kew, London, but they did not include the wall or ceiling detailing. It was evident that the best restoration source would be the burnt out shell, and as such it was crucial to record all that was possible.

BKS Limited of Coleraine were employed to carry out a detailed photogrammetric survey of the Chamber walls and ceiling. Although everything was burnt, sufficient fragments remained to pick up most of the detailing and all the general setting out positions. Accurate scaled photographs were also taken and these proved invaluable.

With the survey complete, further samples were taken down - all the ceiling plaster mouldings, panelling details, column capitals and cladding, remaining sections of seats and metal hand-rails and grilles. Once everything of any value had been removed, the Chamber was cleared back to the bare shell, to allow structural repairs to damaged steelwork and spalled brickwork walls to proceed.

By good fortune the photographer Robert Malone had been commissioned to photograph the Commons Chamber shortly before the fire, and this (sadly) single shot became central to the accurate restoration. The same viewpoint was captured, immediately after the fire, part way through the restoration, and on completion.

The charred ceiling plaster left in place to allow accurate survey drawings and moulds to be made

On 19 April 1995 Sir Patrick Mayhew, then Secretary of State for Northern Ireland, announced to the House of Commons in London that the Government would provide the resources for the complete restoration of the Chamber, in conjunction with the overall upgrading, reservicing and reorganising of the building. Ironically the disaster of the fire brought forward the full restoration and modernisation of the whole building, which had been planned for some years but had been awaiting vacant occupation and allocation of resources. An essential works programme, to deal with upgrading to meet regulations for Health & Safety, disabled access and fire precautions, had already started and this was extended into an enabling works programme to facilitate the main contract.

With such a daunting task ahead, the Construction Service of Department of the Environment Steering Group organised a gathering at the Slieve Donard Hotel of all those to be involved in the project. This was an inspired decision which stimulated the high level of co-ordination and co-operation which characterised the whole work. It was decided to compress the design time to a minimum: tendering was to be on a basis of detailed design drawings and approximate quantities, to be refined as the job progressed. The main contract was awarded to Karl Construction in October 1995, a mere nine months after the fire.

Top left: Sifting through the debris
Top right: The artefact store
Bottom: The public gallery - note survey 'targets' as part of photogrammetric survey

2. IF STONES COULD SPEAK
Stonework cleaning & repairs

In the 1920s teams of Italian masons and their families had moved to Belfast to complete the interior of Parliament Buildings and the Royal Courts of Justice. They left behind a legacy of craftsmanship in travertine, bottocino and other marbles. On returning home they created a Belfast accented, English-speaking population still reputedly recognisable when the 1990s marble masons visited Italy searching for restoration materials. But whereas the natural marbles proved relatively easy to both clean and match, the predominant walling material throughout the ground floor turned out to be an artificial marble, produced in the 'twenties under the trade name of 'Manumarble' but no longer in production. Analysis by Queen's University School of Geosciences revealed it to be 99% marble dust with no obvious binder and presumably cast into slabs under pressure or heat. The tests also revealed the depth of smoke penetration to be minimal - less than 1mm - and the material to be homogeneous.

An extensive testing regime was initiated for all the smoke-stained areas, and Nichola Ashurst, an acknowledged expert on cleaning methods, was employed to advise. With acid and alkali cleaning agents ruled out because of their corrosive effect on marble, testing centred around graffiti removers and degreasing agents, all pH neutral. Whilst these worked on the natural marbles, they made no significant impression on the Manumarble. Meanwhile the architects and the stone contractors had been testing slabs, which had fallen off the walls, for mechanical re-polishing, with excellent results, but there did not seem to be a practical method of cleaning the Manumarble in-situ.

The architects found reference to a low pressure vortex micro particle abrasive cleaning system which had been used with success on delicate terracotta work on the Natural History Museum, London. Trials proved highly impressive, and this system was used for the cleaning of all heavily smoke-damaged areas.

The system proved delicate enough to clean original plaster cornices without eroding the detail, yet sufficiently abrasive to remove all but the most heavily burnt-in stains. The vortex and abrasive air system also cleaned out all the natural hollows and fissures in the travertine, something a chemical based cleaning system would not have done. With replacement Manumarble unavailable it was decided to reclad the first floor level of the Commons Chamber in bottocino (like the Senate Chamber and both circular lobbies) but even then it was evident that a replacement for Manumarble would be required for repairs to corridor areas and after an extensive search Capital Marble of London sourced a similar material. There is now little trace of the fire but here and there a burnt pink edge to a panel gives evidence of the intensity of superheated smoke as 'the honourable scar' of survival and history.

Parliament Buildings was still in its teens when war broke out, and its pristine Portland stone gleaming in the moonlight was an obvious target and landmark for German bombers. The files revealed elaborate plans for suspended camouflage nets but a more pragmatic solution prevailed, and the building was painted - reputedly with tar and cow dung. Stormont never was attacked (shipyards and industry being more valuable targets), and the tar was aggressively removed after the war. The recipe proved resilient and traces still remain today. Being well above the pollutant-laden industrial smogs of the Lagan basin, the stonework has not suffered serious deterioration, and all that was generally required was the application of biocides washed off with low pressure water. A low pressure abrasive cleaning system was selectively used to remove water and pollutant staining around carved work. All this revealed the quality and vibrancy of the original carvings without any loss of detail or sharpness.

The building is of solid masonry construction, with not a single expansion joint: consequently numerous small cracks had opened up at lines of weakness - principally connecting cills and heads of windows. These have all now been repaired with a lime-putty mortar, matching the original material.

It had long been suspected that the front portico had moved or was moving in relation to the building (first mentioned in official files in 1937), and there was direct evidence of two serious problems - at eaves level, where stones had cracked and joints opened up; and at the great stone piers below the balcony, where stones were displaced and heavily water-stained. Extensive monitoring by DOE structural engineers indicated that any historical movement had stopped and that the structure was stable.

Further investigation revealed that the balcony floor had been leaking for years as old asphalt filling between the Portland stone slabs had cracked open. The supporting piers had a brick core which became saturated and expanded, pushing out the facing Portland stone. The problem was serious enough to require many of these stones to be replaced. The entire balcony floor was relaid on a new waterproof membrane and drainage layer.

Left: Ground floor corridor after cleaning and repairs. Top right: External stone cleaning
Middle right: Under wraps - the fully enclosed scaffold that allowed work to go on in all seasons and weather
Bottom right: Repairing the internal stonework

3. SHEDDING LIGHT

Refurbished & supplementary light fittings

A great deal of the character and style of Parliament Buildings is due to its distinctive and distinguished decoration. Whether it be the robust classically-inspired carvings in Portland stone on the exterior of the building, the similar motifs more delicately executed in travertine in the Central Hall, or the fibrous plaster cornicing or carved timber door cases and canopies, this decoration displays influences of the various contemporary styles of the late nineteenth and early twentieth centuries. Anthemions abound along with scrolls, Greek keys, beads and reels, and eggs and darts. Animal skulls are interestingly and less gruesomely interpreted as heavily antlered elk heads, and this particular motif is unique to Parliament Buildings. This palette of decorative elements is whole-heartedly classical and properly used in the architectural grammar of the neo-classical style. However, the influence of Art Nouveau can be seen in the bold, elegant, curved lines of the many other carved features and in the anthemion leaves in particular. There is also a strong resonance of Art Deco throughout the building but nowhere more so than in the very distinctive light fittings installed in the grander Parliamentary accommodation of the ground and first floors.

Whereas standard proprietary glass bowl pendants were used in the upper floors occupied by civil servants, the more elevated officials of Government had their working environment illuminated by very grand bespoke confections of cast glass and bronze. These were designed specifically as part of the building by Arnold Thornely and were manufactured by the General Electric Company.

Left: A classic Stormont fitting with elk's head motif
Top right: Commons Lobby light fitting after the fire
Bottom right: The same fitting, fully restored and back in position

Inside the building there are two families of these Stormont fittings - a circular style, mainly used in the offices and working areas; and an octagonal style, used in corridors and public areas. There are at least fifteen different models within these two styles.

The circular fittings were generally glass hemispherical bowls held in a cast bronze rim, often with a second inverted trumpet-shaped upper glass extending upwards into a decorative boss on a substantial bronze suspension rod. The Elk's head, which occurs throughout the building's decoration, is used in these lights as a fine polished bronze sand-casting attached at three points around the outside of the perimeter ring.

There is a hierarchy within this family of bowl pendants. The lesser fittings are smaller and have fairly plain sand-blasted bowls with a pattern of radiating polished cuts in the glass. The more important fittings are slightly larger and have polished cut crystal bowls.

The fittings of the other principal group are even more interesting, being very distinctive in their arrangement in two tiers, octagonal in shape and a bit like an upside down wedding cake. They comprise flat glass panels suspended in a frame-work of polished bronze glazing bars attached to a decorative cast bronze coronet band. The glass panels are moulded and have a three dimensional low relief pattern of gothic pointed fish scales. The outside surface has a matt finish like coarse sand-blasting but the particular character of the glass comes from a translucent cream colour enamelling applied to the inside surface. These fittings, which are so visually remarkable in themselves, become stunning when they are lit. The colour and texture of the glass panels, the detail of the bronze modelling and the highlights in the polished metal combine to wonderful effect.

60

Left: Octagonal pendant fitting refurbished
Right: Contemporary uplighter, with replicated components based on the original octagonal lights

In particular individual locations there are very special fittings developed from these two families, most notably the very large bowl pendants in the circular lobbies on the approaches to the Chambers; the octagonal bulkhead fittings with curved, flaring and highly modelled upper glasses, in the north-south corridors, and also outside the Chambers; and the squarish fittings in the Members' Dining Room which incorporate air extract ducts.

Also notable are the spectacular octagonal lanterns in the south entrance portico, once again the same family but scaled up to the robust proportions of the exterior of the building.

However remarkable are the building's bespoke fittings, the most special of all are the five grand chandeliers of the Central Hall. The large central one was originally a gift from Kaiser Wilhelm to the Royal family. The four minor companions were designed to complement it and were crafted by local tradesmen using carved wood and gesso plaster in place of the cast metal of the original.

The refurbishment of the building required that levels of illumination be improved to modern standards, while maintaining the most efficient use of energy and meeting the statutory requirements for emergency lighting. This, along with the need to remove accumulated dirt, to repair any damage incurred during sixty-five years use and to check the structural condition of these old fabrications, necessitated an extensive scheme to attend to every fitting individually.

Each one was surveyed in its location, tagged and removed to the workshops of Dernier and Hamlyn in London. In a way this closed some sort of circle, as this firm is perhaps the only one lighting manufacturer remaining since before the turn of the century when they built similar fittings for Belfast City Hall, the Technical Institute at College Square, Belfast, and even for the great ocean liners such as the Pendennis Castle and the Arlanza built by Harland and Wolff in Belfast.

Every component was individually cleaned and re-assembled, and new parts were made as exact replicas where replacement was necessary. This was not too difficult for the metal bits, but the arcane craft of making new cast glass panels was more of a problem. After some considerable searching Jeff Bell, an artisan working in Dalston in the east end of London, was found still to have the skills not only to cast the glass but also to apply the translucent enamelling. (This colourful character delivered his work in a hearse!) The new panels are virtually indistinguishable from the originals.

Modern lamps are brighter, much more efficient, but unfortunately very different in shape and size from the original tungsten filament bulbs. Many fittings also now have to accommodate additional emergency lamps. Much of the skill in the refurbishment has been in devising neat and discreet ways of integrating new equipment whilst retaining the same character. A combination of painstaking design, trial, error and ingenuity has allowed this to happen.

But even with these improvements some altogether new fittings had to be introduced. Uplighters, unheard of in 1930, but commonplace today, were devised to give a better spread of light throughout offices. Their style is based on the original octagonal lights, using the same cast bronze work to produce very impressive, six foot tall, free-standing units.

The Central Hall's chandeliers were always impressive but, now restored, they are magnificent. Impossible to reach for regular cleaning, they had accumulated grime since first put in place. They were taken down, the large one disassembled, and all were removed to London where each part was meticulously cleaned. They were then rewired and had new lamp holders and candle tubes fitted. The substance and quality of the original chandelier meant that not much repair was required.

64

Not so the four minor pieces whose construction, however admirably executed by the original tradesmen, had used less durable materials of wood and gesso, much of which was disintegrating. Dernier and Hamlyn cast in metal new brackets and delicate filigree rims to the drip pans, close replicas of their predecessors, and these were fitted to the original bosses. They should now last for ever.

In order that they can be maintained in their pristine grandeur, all these chandeliers have been re-hung on electric winches concealed within the ceiling and they can now be lowered easily and safely for regular dusting and relamping.

The light now sparkles through cut crystal drip pans which were previously unrecognisable as glass, and the superb ceiling has regained a brilliance not fully appreciable for very many years.

Left: The restored main chandelier in the Central Hall
Top right: The chandelier illuminates the brilliance of the magnificent ceiling
Bottom Left: A kit of parts - the chandelier during restoration

4. NEW WINE IN OLD BOTTLES
Re-ordering the layout for new uses

Few buildings are able to fulfil for ever the functions for which they were originally designed. Particularly in the twentieth century, during which the way we live has changed more and faster than at any other time in history, the need for buildings to adapt to change is greater than ever.

The ability to absorb change is perhaps fundamental to whether buildings survive as living working entities or whether they become functionally anachronistic, their interest and value lying purely in their architecture or their history. However valuable they are from these perspectives, it is even better to have them alive and taking their part in life and continuing history.

Success in carrying out refurbishment or restoration in old and important buildings is often measured by the degree of intervention. Changes should be imperceptible in that they are either buried in the original form or, if visible, are carried out within a complementary ethos.

This principle has underwritten all of the refurbishment work at Parliament Buildings. The areas where physical change has been necessary relate mainly to the shortcomings of the original building in satisfying the new demands of holding state functions, either in the execution of government business or for the promotion of the region's trade and commercial interests. Similarly, the original kitchens and staff canteens located on the fourth floor were inconvenient and archaic and had become inefficient due to the lack of support from those for whom they were intended.

Reorganisation of catering and reception facilities entailed providing new kitchens in a more convenient location in the basement, at the same time creating there a new, up-to-date restaurant to serve staff and public alike. Upstairs, a new suite of reception rooms was added to augment the original Members', Dining and Conference Rooms, extending along the entire first floor frontage and comprising a coffee room, a small private dining room, a bar and, perhaps most striking of all, the Long Gallery.

These are all significant alterations to the building and are unquestionably a response to the needs of the late twentieth century. They have therefore been designed honestly, as contemporary additions complementary to the style of Thornely's original architecture.

The basement restaurant, uncompromisingly contemporary, was formed by carrying out major and technically difficult structural modifications to form a series of very large arches through one of the main load-bearing masonry walls. The arches are expressive of the great weight and substance of the building above by being low and squat, and supported on short, very robustly proportioned circular columns which give a cellar-like ambience. However, there is no cellar-like gloom, as the most is made of the original high-level semi-basement windows which are south facing and admit as much daylight as possible. In order to make the most of this light, the colour scheme chosen is based on warm and sunny colours, and the effect has been to create an atmosphere which is proving as welcoming, comfortable and popular as any modern restaurant, quite unlike that of the original staff canteen on the fourth floor.

Left: The new restaurant in the basement. Top right: The new bar on the first floor
Bottom right: A new Ladies' toilet after the style of the original Gentlemen's toilets

One of the principal offices on the first floor, formerly the Prime Minister's Room

70

On the first floor a more refined and less populist, but no less popular, approach has been taken. The private dining room is strikingly decorated with damask wall panels within moulded plaster work featuring a simple tulip design in a modern William Morris theme by the local interior designer Alison Vance. This superb fabric, which is also used for the Roman window blinds, was specially woven by Glenanne Jacquards in County Armagh.

Whereas this room and its adjoining anteroom were original apartments, not so the bar which has been created by bringing three rooms together into a single five-bay space. The most striking feature here is the dado-height diagonally-arranged quarter-veneered oak wall panelling, and again developed in the detailing of the bar counter. This panelling is a replica of that used by Thornely in the original Strangers' Dining Room. The interior decoration, again by Alison Vance, is redolent of the 'thirties with subtle jazz age overtones in the carpet pattern appropriate to the period of the building's origin and, at the same time, contemporary. Again, the carpet was locally designed and manufactured, to the highest levels of quality, by Ulster Carpet Mills, Portadown who also produced bespoke carpets for all ground and first floor rooms, to designs by the architects, reflecting the classical motifs of the building.

The Long Gallery is the most important of the new additions. For some considerable time the need to hold large functions had necessitated the use of the Central Hall as no other large space was available, but this had been neither appropriate nor comfortable. In order to address this need the Long Gallery was conceived. Three offices, the original Strangers' Dining Room, and the serving kitchen which had inappropriately occupied four bays of the most important south front elevation, were converted into one space over 130 feet long by 18 feet wide. Given a space of this proportion, it could become nothing other than 'The Long Gallery'.

The new private Dining Room on the first floor

PARLIAMENT BUILDINGS, STORMONT
1922 - 1998

The room was designed to be a forthright, contemporary addition to the building, and the temptation to produce a pretence of the original by copying was resisted. Good architecture is polite to its neighbours, and in deference to the rest of the building the design is based on classical principles using the existing fenestration to establish a rhythm of columns, pilasters and beams. A palette of materials was established based on bottocino marble, oak timber and bronze metalwork as originally used elsewhere in the building. The stone was carved using a simple Greek key design on the face of pilasters, again as a reference to some of the original classical decoration. New pendant light fittings were designed in a contemporary style, but again using the same glass and bronze materials and a simplified form of the decoration used in the original fittings.

In concert with French craftsmen a spectacular oak parquet floor was designed, based on floors used in the great French palaces such as Versailles and the Louvre. Beams from a chateau in central France were reclaimed using ancient craft skills. Every piece of the intricate parquetry was individually cut and shaped, and assembled using only timber pins with no nails and no glue!

Arranged in nine bays, the wall panels, in rich Venetian red plaster, are intended to accommodate a collection of paintings, for which a bronze picture-hanging rail system has been provided.

The room is of its own time but fits comfortably and with no element of shock into the building.

The Long Gallery

5. THE COMMONS CHAMBER

Restoration & extension

For over forty years the Commons Chamber of Parliament Buildings was the centre of political power in Northern Ireland. In a Chamber laid out in an adversarial style modelled on Westminster, the Unionist government faced its disparate and minority opposition across the central table in front of the Speaker's chair, until direct rule was imposed in 1972. In the hope of ameliorating the verbal battleground of directly facing and opposing parties, the seating was changed into a horseshoe plan for the short-lived Assemblies of 1972 and 1982/86 (thereby interrupting the processional route through the length of the building, from the Speaker's Chair in the Commons via the Central Hall to the Senate Chamber). Sir Patrick Mayhew authorised the restoration of the Chamber, but, in the absence of political agreement on the size and form of a new parliamentary body, the seating pattern was not decided until after the 1998 Assembly came into being.

Although a proper restoration of the main features of the Chamber after the fire was of primary importance, the opportunity was taken in addition to correct the main failings of the original layout. These were, principally, the inadequate accommodation for public visitors and the press; no provision for disabled access for either; and minimal facilities for media and staff commentators and technicians to control sound, television monitoring, and recording of proceedings. The design team visited Westminster to understand fully the requirements of the technical staff and the practicalities of operating a parliamentary building. Further research was carried out on new or refurbished parliamentary buildings in Edinburgh, Dublin and Brussels.

Two crucial decisions were taken which allowed the design team to solve all the practical problems.

1. The creation of side galleries above the ground floor voting lobbies, thus turning the Chamber into a four-sided amphitheatre and doubling the visitor seating. A further level above the galleries and the Chamber roof void now houses the new air-handling plant. These new galleries allow fire escape in two directions and provide level disabled access from the corridor at the west end to a designated wheelchair space at the end of each gallery.

2. The forming of two television monitor/sound control rooms at the original east end gallery, partly from former toilets, partly from the rear gallery area. These overlook almost the whole floor area of the Chamber and are fully sound-proofed with one-way glass viewing panels.

Once the physical shape had been decided, the fitting-out proposals were developed. A high level of totally flexible servicing was required to cater for almost any seating layout and this has been fully integrated into the structure. With the side galleries in place the old window walls were opened up and the former demi-columns became free-standing full columns. Structural requirements meant that the original steelwork had to be re-cased, but this was kept to a minimum to avoid sight lines being restricted. The elaborate window surrounds were reconstructed, based on surviving fragments and pre-fire photographs.

The BKS photogrammetric survey proved its worth, determining time and again the complex and rigidly symmetrical setting inside a structure which was anything but square. The ceiling was perhaps the most complex problem. Once the twisted steelwork had been braced and some new sections added, the carcassing was installed to support the elaborate cornices and beams.

Again it was discovered that the structural frame was neither square nor symmetrical, and it proved an almost impossible task to allow for the differences between adjoining bays and at the same time line up on the beam soffits. Careful scrutiny will reveal how such a regular appearance was achieved against a background of fire-distorted light grilles and unequal bay divisions. (The clues are visible for those who might wish to be distracted from the tedium of parliamentary proceedings!)

With the ceiling plasterwork complete attention turned to the decoration. A close examination of the Central Hall ceiling showed that the gold and silver had been laid on in both leaf and powder forms tailored to the type of gilding most appropriate to each moulding.

Over a period of six months Hyndman Milliken painstakingly carried out the gilding almost single-handed, and the result is a testament to both his skill and patience.

A prominent feature of the Chamber had been the matched quarter crown-cut walnut veneered panelling from floor to gallery level, finished with an ebony inlaid Greek key pattern frieze. Above that the veneers to balustrades, doors and panelling were straight-cut set in diamond or diagonal patterns. Those same principles were used in the restoration, though there were some changes at gallery level to accommodate the new side galleries and building control requirements for balustrades. Sourcing the walnut was a problem - the only English walnut logs available were pre-purchased lest they be lost, but the sheer quantity required meant also using French supplies. It was somewhat gratifying to learn that no machine-moulded carving could match the quality or complexity or the originals, and every piece of carved work has now been hand carved again.

Left: The Commons Chamber under reconstruction with the new side galleries
Right: Gilding work in progress

78

Left: The Commons Chamber completed
Right: Doorcase and column capital

Left: The new side galleries
Right: View along a side gallery

Client:

Office Accommodation Branch - Department of the Environment, Northern Ireland

Design Team:

Project Managers: DOE Construction Service

Architects: Consarc Design Group

Interior Design: Consarc Design Group & Alison Vance Interiors

Quantity Surveyors: DOE Construction Service & Consarc Design Group

Mechanical & Electrical Engineers: Building Design Partnership (BDP)

Structural Engineers: DOE Construction Service

Landscape Architects: DOE Construction Service

Support Services:

DOE Construction Service: Clerks of Works; Fire Safety; Building Control

DOE: Supplies Branch; Catering

DOE Environment & Heritage Service: Protecting Historic Buildings

Department of National Heritage, London

The Clerk to the Assembly

Building Research Establishment (BRE)

Adriel Consultants

THE RESTORATION TEAM

Construction Team:

Main Contractor: KARL Construction Limited

Electrical Contractor: Blackbourne Electrical Company Limited
Mechanical Contractors: Vaughan Mechanical Services;
Blackbourne Mechanical
Historic Lighting Sub-contractor: Dernier & Hamlyn

Joinery Sub-contractors: O'Neill Bros; Ramseys Limited

Stonework & Marble: George Cunningham & Co

Marble & Terrazzo: D. McAuley & Sons

Fibrous Plasterwork: Georgian Design; Belfast Mould Company

Painting: N.I. Coatings Limited

Specialist Cleaning: A.B. Cleaning; C.I.F. Limited

Gilding: Hyndman Milliken

French Polishing: Drummond Reid

Floor Finishes: Floorform Limited

Specialist Metalwork: J.L. Ornamental Castings

Metal Windows & Specialist Glass: W.F.M. Limited

Bespoke Carpets: Ulster Carpet Mills

Specialist Fabrics: Glenanne Jacquards Limited

Long Gallery Floor: Agora; Les Parquets Francais

Roofing: Grainger Bros. Limited

Sash Window Refurbishment: Ventrolla (Ireland) Limited

Cladding: EDM CECO; Kingspan Limited

Textile Restoration: Catherine McClintock

Catering Equipment: Stephens Catering

Commons Gallery Seating: Audience Systems Limited

Venetian Plaster: Armourcoat Limited

Lifts: Express Lifts; Adair Bros. Limited

Also the many other contractors, suppliers,
manufacturers and installers who all played their part
in the restoration process and prior enabling works.

The restoration team, 1996

[Hussey, Christopher] 'The Government of Northern Ireland's new Parliament Building at Belfast', in *Country life*, Vol. 72, 1932, p.356 (September)

Ulster Parliament Buildings, Commemorative volume by Wm Stewart & Partners, November 1932

'The Parliament Building, Northern Ireland', in *The builder*, November 11, 1932, pp. 806-7; November 18, 1932, p.812

XQ *The truth about Stormont: more of Northern Ireland's "Mad finance"*. Belfast, [Irish News], January 1933

Dixon, Hugh *An introduction to Ulster architecture*. Belfast, UAHS, 1975, p.82

Oliver, J A *Working at Stormont*. Dublin, Institute of Public Administration, 1978, p.133

Shea, Patrick *Voices and the sound of drums*. Belfast, Blackstaff Press, 1981, p.115

Parliament Buildings, Stormont. Belfast, HMSO, 1985

Larmour, Paul *Belfast: an architectural guide*. Belfast, Friar's Bush Press, 1987, pp.109-111

Nicks, H 'Stormont Castle: history and architecture', in *East Belfast Historical Society journal*, Vol. 2, no.3, November 1988, pp.14-20

Stewart, Anne M *Irish art societies and sketching clubs: index of exhibitions 1870-1980*. Vol. 1. Dublin, Four Courts Press, 1997

The Public Record Office of Northern Ireland contains miscellaneous documents and files relating to the fabric of Parliament Buildings and the Speaker's House, covering the period 1924-1944 (CWPB). The Monuments and Buildings Record at Hill Street, Belfast, maintains files on Parliament Buildings and on the Stormont estate (D/063).

ACKNOWLEDGEMENTS

Contemporary Photographs: Christopher Hill Photographic
DOE Construction Service
Consarc Design Group

Historic Photographs: Album of photographs taken during construction 1924-1927,
presented to the Prime Minister, Sir James Craig, by the
contractors, Wm Stewart & Partners
(Northern Ireland Assembly Library, Stormont, E6/51).
Other similar or selective versions of this album
were presented to a few Government officials.
There is a copy in the Public Record Office of
Northern Ireland, CWPB/1

Ulster Museum, R J Welch collection, W10/70/11 - p.15
Courtesy of Trustees of the National Museums and Galleries of Northern Ireland

J Nelson McMillen Esq CBE - Foundation stone photograph - p.16
Courtesy of the late Mr McMillen's daughter

The truth about Stormont (Irish News) 1933 - Perspective - p.21

Text: Text written by John Kennedy, George Woodman,
Belinda Jupp, William Mol, Dawson Stelfox,
and edited by Gordon Wheeler.

The Ulster Architectural Heritage Society would like to thank
the following for their assistance in checking details:
Dr Eileen Black of the Ulster Museum; Karen Latimer and
Michael Smallman of the Queen's University Library; and the
staff of the Northern Ireland Assembly Library. The passages
quoted on p.43 are reproduced by kind permission of Blackstaff Press
and the Institute of Public Administration, Dublin, respectively.

Book design and layout by Alison Gault Design and Illustration.

Back Cover: *Capstone from Main Gate pillar*